The Argument of Alexander Wedderburn, Esq; His Majesty's Solicitor General, in the Cause of Lord Pomfret Against Smith; Which was Tried at the bar of the Court of King's-Bench, Westminster

Elizabeth Lumbley

To be left till calld for
at the post offis — — — york

THE

ARGUMENT

OF

ALEXANDER WEDDERBURN, Esq;

HIS MAJESTY'S SOLICITOR GENERAL,

IN THE

CAUSE

OF

LORD POMFRET *against* SMITH;

Which was tried at the Bar of the Court of King's-Bench, Westminster;

Before LORD CHIEF JUSTICE MANSFIELD, and MR. JUSTICE WILLES,

On Saturday the 7th, and Monday the 9th of November 1772;

BY A

SPECIAL JURY OF THE COUNTY OF YORK,

On the following Issue directed by the Court of Chancery, viz.

"*Whether the Ground within the Manor of Healaugh, in Swaledale, in*
"*the County of York, lying and being between a certain Place there*
"*called Swinnergill and a Place called East Gill, (in which the Lead*
"*Mine in Dispute is situate) be Part of the Commons or Wastes of*
"*the said Manor, or not?*"

On which Issue a VERDICT was found for Mr. SMITH, "*that the*
"*said Ground was not, nor is, Part of the Wastes of the said Manor.*"

PRINTED in the YEAR M,DCC,LXXIII.

ADVERTISEMENT.

THE following speech makes its appearance under very considerable disadvantages.—To do it justice, it would be necessary to print that of the Attorney-General, (who opened lord *Pomfret*'s cause,) and also the evidence produced on the part of his lordship, as well as the remainder of the trial: this was originally intended, but the design was afterwards dropped, as it would have produced a folio volume, and greatly added to the immense expence with which Mr *Smith* has been loaded during the progress of his contest with lord *Pomfret*; this must serve as an apology to Mr Solicitor-General, as several parts of the following speech have allusions to his opponent's arguments, and to facts, which arose in the former part of the trials, allusions that had great force and beauty in the delivery, but which must, in a great measure, be lost to those who had not the pleasure of hearing them.—The speaker did ample justice to the subject; he fully exerted those great powers for which he is so justly distinguished; he was thoroughly acquainted with the series of hardships Mr *Smith* had sustained in defence of his property, after a peaceable possession of more than thirty years; and was sensible that lord *Pomfret*, or his agents, had made use of every method, (which the practice of the courts but too well enabled him) to delay, harrass, and if possible, ruin Mr *Smith* by repeated applications to the courts below, upon every trivial occasion, and by presenting no less than three Appeals to the House of Lords, in the course of two years, which were attended with an enormous expence, and for which Mr. Smith never did, nor could, receive the least compensation.

T, E

THE firſt trial, in 1770, though had at *York*, (and where Mr *Smith* alſo obtained a verdict,) neceſſarily occaſioned a vaſt expence, but on lord *Pomfret*'s inſiſting in 1772, to try the queſtion over again, at bar, the difficulties and expences Mr *Smith* was laid under were prodigiouſly encreaſed. He had all his witneſſes, many of whom were very aged and infirm, to collect from diſtant parts of the counties of *York*, *Weſtmoreland*, and *Cumberland*, and bring them to *London*, at an inclement ſeaſon of the year.—Mr Solicitor-General, from a conſideration of theſe circumſtances, entered heartily and warmly into the ſubject, of which he ſhewed himſelf to be complete maſter, he detected every fallacy, that had been offered in argument, he developed and expoſed every falſe fact, that was endeavored to be eſtabliſhed by evidence, and, though he was refuſed the inſpection of ſome pieces of written evidence, which Mr *Chaytor* produced at the *cloſe* of the firſt day, imagining they would have given a *coup de grace* to the cauſe, yet Mr Solicitor, not only obviated the force of any concluſions, which the other ſide had, with amazing confidence, drawn from theſe papers, but ſhewed to the ſatisfaction of the court, that, on a fair examination of them, they were the ſtrongeſt and moſt concluſive evidence for Mr *Smith*, nay, to ſuch a degree, that (ſtrange as it may ſeem) even his lordſhip's agents were *ſhamed* of the production, and endeavoured to ſhift the blame of it from one to the other. Mr *Chaytor*, however, had been ſo ſanguine in his opinion of their importance, that, long before the trial, he declared they would be deciſive of the queſtion.

THEY were equally unfortunate in their other piece of *written* evidence, —they produced the accounts of Mr *Cloſe* the receiver, to ſupport and ſubſtantiate the evidence of a ſet of men, who were brought to prove that they had, for a courſe of years after Mr *Smith*'s purchaſe, got ore from a certain part of the ground in queſtion, as being part of the waſtes of the manor, but when theſe accounts came to be inſpected and compared with the authentic documents of the very truſt agents themſelves, the fact turned out quite the reverſe, for the accounts proved to demonſtration, that theſe witneſſes were, at the time they swore to, working in the *wastes*, at a very considerable distance from the place in question.—Though this piece of evidence was not found by Mr *Clayton* in *Pandora's box* at *Windsor*, yet, from a similarity of circumstances, it may be presumed it was his *happy* discovery

In such a contrariety of *vivâ voce* evidence it would have been very difficult for any jury to have distinguished truth from falsehood, unless they had previously viewed the place in question, this had been done by the juries who tried both causes, they were all gentlemen of the first character and property in the County of *York*, they chearfully submitted to the inconvenience and fatigue of coming from very distant parts of it, into a rude country, for the single purpose of doing justice between the parties, and the last jury willingly undertook a journey to *London*, in the winter season, sat with the greatest patience, and strictest attention, near fourteen hours each day of the trial, without the least refreshment, and, after it was over, and they were informed that lord *Pomfret*'s solicitor had receded from an agreement, made in court, for payment of a moiety of their expences, &c they very generously accepted from Mr *Smith*, a sum not equal to their travelling charges

Mr Smith enjoyed his victory a very short time, but his representative is now in the peaceable possession of this mine, and however much Mr *Smith*'s estate may have suffered from this long and very expensive contest, yet he receives the singular satisfaction, and the event of this cause has shewn, that, while the noble institution of Juries continues in this country, it will not be possible for any one, however exalted in rank, or countenanced or supported by power, to make depredations on his fellow subjects with impunity, or ultimately succeed in any plan formed against their property, which has not truth and justice for its support.

The

The Names of the Special Jury who tried the Cause, at the Assizes at *York*, on *Friday* the 10th, and *Saturday* the 11th, of *August* 1770.

Sir Digby Legard, of *Ganton*, Bart.
Peter Conset, of *Knayton-cum-Brawith*, Esq;
Gregory Elsley, of *Fillifkirk*, Esq,
Simon Butterwick, of *Thirsk*, Esq,
Gregory Elsley, Jun of *Patrick Brumpton*, Esq;
Mark Milbank, of *Barningham*, Esq,
Walter Hawksworth, of *Hawksworth*, Esq,
Benjamin Ferrand, of *St Ives*, Esq,
Walter Vavasor, of *Weston*, Esq,
James Maude, of *Leathley*, Esq;
Roger Swire, of *Farnley-cum-Conningly*, Esq;
Robert Belt, of *Buttercromb*, Esq,

The Names of the Special Jury of the County of *York*, who tried the same Cause at the Bar of the Court of *King's-Bench* at *Westminster*, on *Saturday* the 7th, and *Monday* the 9th of *November*, 1772.

Sir Bellingham Graham, of *Norton Conyers*, Bart.
Francis Smith of *Kirby Knowle*, Esq,
Stephen Croft, the younger, of *Stillington*, Esq,
Wilmer Gosip, of *Upper Helmsley*, Esq,
John Sawrey Morritt, of *Rokeby*, Esq,
Randolph Marriot, of *Aysgough*, Esq,
Henry Wickham, of *Cottingley*, Esq,
Peter Wilson Overend, of *Bentham*, Esq,
Edward Foxcroft, of *Thornton-with-Burton*, Esq,
Joshua Field, of *Heaton-with-Clayton*, Esq,
Robert Grimston, of *Beeford*, Esq,
Robert Gee, of *Bishop Burton*, Esq,

Mr.

Mr. Solicitor General's

ARGUMENT.

Gentlemen of the Jury,

I Am glad that an opportunity has been given me to request your *fresh* * attention to the stating of an entire new case my learned friend, who opened this cause on the part of Lord Pomfret, had too much judgment, in stating his Lordship's case, to open to you any circumstances of that of Mr Smith, of which you remain at present in ignorance, and I am convinced that no prepossession can dwell in any mind, with regard to a case of which they have not yet heard one circumstance disclosed I have therefore to beg of you, gentlemen, to favor me with your indulgence, while I lay what I have to say before you in the following order

* *This cause began at eight o'clock on Saturday morning, the whole day was taken up in opening Lord Pomfret's case and examining his witnesses, at ten o'clock at night, Lord Mansfield directed Mr Smith's counsel to open his defence, and although the jury had sat fourteen hours without the least refreshment, and though Mr Smith's witnesses (most of them very ancient) were tired out with so long an attendance, it was with the greatest difficulty they could prevail to have it put off to Monday Morning.*

I will first state to you the defendant's case, as if this was the opening of a new cause, I will then go into an examination of the evidence you heard the other day and close with stating to you the evidence that will be adduced on the part of the defendant in answer to that evidence, so far as it is necessary to be answered, and in order to establish the case of Mr Smith, upon a ground totally distinct from any part of that evidence

It has been stated to you, gentlemen, that the estate, which gives rise to this suit, was originally the property of the duke of Wharton The disorder of that nobleman's affairs produced, so early as the year 1722, a deed, by which he conveyed all his estates to trustees, to be sold for the payment of his debts The estate was taken into the management of the trustees a bill was brought by the creditors for the execution of that trust in the court of chancery, and long before the duke's death, a receiver was appointed by that court, for the management of the estate The cause lasted a great while, a great number of creditors was to come in and prove debts, and no steps were taken for the sale of the estate, till after the attainder of the duke Upon that event, the Crown was pleased to grant to Lady Jane Coke, and Lady Lucy Morris, the duke's sisters, the reversion of the estate, after payment of debts It turned out in fact, that there was nothing left of the estate but what was produced from the mines In 1733, Mr Close was appointed the receiver the cause was carried on, and directions were given for the sale of the estates In 1737 and 1738, the estates were sold and you will be pleased, gentlemen, to attend to this circumstance, that all that in fact remained to the family, all the expectations they could entertain of any thing beneficial from the grant, were founded upon the prospect of *mines*, for every inch of landed property was sold, and the produce entirely consumed in the payment of debts I speak of known facts, there was nothing left, nay, there were classes of creditors unsatisfied, and some of those postponed creditors, even since I attended the bar, have received a satisfaction out of part of the produce of these mines Gentlemen, I point out this observation to you, because you will not think

think it possible, when he [illegible] the [illegible] to which the family looked, that the disposition of the farms, the description of them, the possession given, should have been circumstances carelessly attended to, or negligently transacted.

In 1738 Mr Smith purchased the Manors of *Healaugh* and *Muker*, and some of the farms that lay within these manors, which the family of Wharton held in Swaledale. The manors consisted of considerable farms, and among others, of *Crackpot Hall farm*. It was then let at 20l. a year, and was described to be in the occupation of *Simon Harker*. You will find by the evidence, that 20l. had been the rent of the farm for above fifty years before the purchase, and for thirty years since there never has been an advance of the rent. In the year 1770, Mr Smith employed an improving agent to look over the estates, and even then, with all the advantages of the rise of rent, that farm was raised to, and is now let at only 26l. In 1738 Mr Smith was let into the possession of the estate by Mr. Close the receiver, who had lived all his life time in the neighbourhood, and than whom no man had a better knowledge of the Wharton estate. he had been engaged as a considerable mine agent: from 1733 he had been the agent and receiver of this very estate, he could not possibly be ignorant of the extent and situation of it, and he could not be partial to Mr Smith considering that he remained no agent for him, but he did remain an agent for the duke's sisters and the only estate in which he could be an agent for *them*, was the mines that were reserved. It has been said, Mr Smith saw the estate about the time of the purchase, if he did so, I believe he has never seen it since, and tho' he is a man of property in Yorkshire, I am certain he is totally unknown to any of you: he has for many years lived a recluse life, scarcely stirring out of his chambers in Gray's-Inn, almost entirely secluded from society, and, if it is possible to quote an instance of one man more singularly negligent of his affairs than another, it is Mr Smith.

LORD

Lord Mansfield, then he muſt be either very rich, or very poor

Mr. Solicitor-General. Or very indolent—Gentlemen, I ſpeak of well-known facts, there is not a man in the world ſo ſingularly inattentive to his own concerns; nay, the very diſcovery of this mine (ſo much the favourite object of Lord Pomfret) was to him a matter of concern, as it involved him in this vexatious and expenſive conteſt.*

In 1738 the purchaſe was made, poſſeſſion was delivered. The purchaſe deed contained in it two reſervations, one was of all mines within the *waſtes* or *commons*, the other was of all ſubſiſting bargains in any part of the eſtate during their continuance. You have already heard from one of the witneſſes, and alſo from Mr. Attorney General, in his opening, that there was a bargain to one Fryar then ſubſiſting on the place in queſtion, and a trial making on *Beldy Hill*, the very place where the mine has been ſince diſcovered, Mr Smith could not therefore immediately upon his purchaſe take any poſſeſſion by mining in the ground in queſtion, which on one ſide is called *Hall Moor*, on the other the *Hall*, or *Out Paſture* In 1742, when the ſubſiſting bargains were worn out, and the hopes of new adventurers were excited that mines might be diſcovered in Mr. Smith's eſtate, an application was made to him by Hartley and Parke he let to them a leaſe, for twenty-one years, of a liberty to ſearch for mines within his eſtate, this paſture was excepted in that leaſe. In 1743 they applied for a leaſe including this paſture, and Mr. Smith granted them one for the ſame term as the former leaſe in which it had been excepted In this ſecond leaſe, Mr. Smith granted them a liberty of ſearching for mines under the paſture *commonly called Crackpot Hall Out Paſture*. There would have been very little in this, if Hartley and Parke had not, as ſoon as they got this leaſe, immediately entered into poſſeſſion They

* *Mr. Smith out-lived this trial but a few months: he had, however, the ſatisfaction of dying in quiet poſſeſſion of the mines in queſtion.*

broke

broke ground at Baldy Hill, ſunk ſhafts, and dug for ore there: they carried on their workings in every year to 1747 There I ſtop, becauſe it is a period at which I muſt ſtate very particularly what happened During the above years, they worked openly and viſibly, and not with a few men, the feweſt were four, ſometimes the number extended to twenty or thirty They had occaſion very early in their trials to make a croſs cut, which was carried a conſiderable length, and made at a conſiderable expence What were the agents of the truſt eſtate, and particularly Mr Cloſe, doing at this time? Were they ignorant, or at a diſtance from them? So much the reverſe, they were working mines for the benefit of the truſt eſtate on the other ſide *Swinnergill Beck*, in a conſtant intercourſe with the different miners, and in a daily knowledge of the leſſees works

Having thus gone on for ſome time, and failed in their firſt attempt at Baldy Hill, the trial was deſerted there, and in 1747, they betook themſelves to that ſide of the ground next Swinnergill Beck, which was ſtill nearer, nay even cloſe to the truſt mines In 1747, the agents, who were carrying on the mines for Lady Jane Coke, began to attend to the works carrying on by Mr Smith's leſſees, becauſe they were then carried on in ſuch a direction, and ſo near, that it was neceſſary to ſee that they did not extend into the truſt liberties Application was therefore made (as was natural the mines being ſo contiguous) for leave to go down into the mines of Hartley and Parke to examine them, not under any idea that Cloſe had a right to interrupt their workings, but merely as a matter of favor After an examination of the mines on both ſides, the directions that Cloſe gave to the miners working on the truſt eſtate, were, that they ſhould take care to keep their workings on the truſt ſide of Swinnergill Beck, ſo as not to go beyond the ſtone wall or boundary, that when their workings approached near *that* line, they ſhould diſl in their reſpective mines Mr Cloſe himſelf had not only marked out the boundaries above ground, but he was ſo perfectly acquainted with the ſeveral rights of the parties, that he ſtated to the different miners the boundaries below ground, pointed out their ſeveral rights, and gave directions to

each

each party not to carry the works beyond their respective boundaries

Gentlemen, this is not all, though that circumstance alone would be very strong, but it happened at that time that though the mines, which were working there for the trust estate, afforded no actual advantage, yet there were considerable prospects Mr Close therefore employed his field agents to examine from time to time, and make him weekly reports, not only of the actual state of their own workings, but of the general condition of the ground, and to make observations upon the bearings and directions of the several veins of ore in the lessees works on the opposite side of the Beck, and to see that each kept within their own boundaries But it was not merely for these purposes that the field agents were employed by Close, there was a further view It was conceived, that the workings carrying on by Hartley and Parke, would drain the works on the other side, by means of the level they would make, and enable Close to carry on his works by means of such level, his agents went therefore to view the state of Hartley and Parkes's work, in order to judge when it would be proper to commence their own

Of this operation, as well as the other, weekly reports were made by the field-agents to Mr Close, and at last, in the month of September 1747, they reported to him, that, from the condition of Hartley and Parkes's works, it was probable their level would soon have the effect to clear the mines on the other side, and that then it would be prudent for them to begin their own works They were not mistaken in their conjecture, for the effect followed, and in a few weeks after the level had been carried to a certain pitch by Hartley and Parkes the trust agents and miners began their own works, and got lead to a considerable value, by means of that very level

Gentlemen, if I was to rest here, I should think my cause sufficiently fortified, with regard to the state and condition of this ground, at the time of Mr Smith's purchase For if from 1738 to 1748, the first ten years after his possession, the agents of the trust estate, who must

must be acquainted with the nature of this property, in every respect, had admitted his right, had availed themselves of the workings under his right, not for the purpose of disturbing or interrupting him, but in order to work their own mines to advantage, shall we in 1772, be deemed better judges than Mr Close, or the trust agents, of the condition of that property? But, gentlemen, it does not rest even here, I have stronger facts to state to you, than those I have opened —

When Hartley and Parkes had carried on these works from 1747 to 1750, they began to find that the *expence* of getting was greater than the *profits* arising from the lead they found, they therefore, in 1750, came to a determination to abandon those workings. The consequence of which was this, it was in the power of Hartley and Parkes, by stopping, or breaking their own level, to drown the mines on the trust estate, and it was very fully their intention to do it, you may say it was unneighbourly, certainly it was so, but I believe it was that kind of conduct that opposite miners use to each other, for, if they cannot get, they do not chuse their neighbours should Hartley and Parkes adopted this idea; and they gave notice to the agents of the trust estate, that they should let the water into their level, and drown their own mine, the consequence might have been, not only to have drowned the mine on the other side, but the miners also the notice was therefore given, that the men might take care of themselves *Close* was much alarmed at this, his mine was prosperous, and it was of great convenience to have the benefit of this level, and to prevent the mine being drowned

Hartley and Parkes began their operation, and as they drew their water from what is called a race, which arose from a place confessedly part of the commons and beyond the northern boundary of the pasture, Close, when he had notice that the lessees intended to destroy the level and drown their mine, gave their directions to his agents, in order to frustrate the scheme he directed them to go and cut the water off from above where Hartley and Parkes had a right to break ground,

ground, and to draw it off by a drain before it flowed into the pasture, and thus to prevent its coming into the mine, and he particularly instructed them to cut it off upon the moor, beyond the northern fence of the pasture in dispute, and for this clear express reason, because *within* the fence he had no right to break ground, but beyond that fence, which was common and waste, he had a right to make any trenches for the purpose of his mine his directions, I repeat it, were —" Go upon the moor, intercept the water before it comes " into the pasture, but go beyond the northern fence of the pasture, " and if we can draw off the water there, we have a right to do it " They went by Close's direction, they cut the water race upon the moor, close to the northern boundary, which he described as the fence of the pasture and by this means they diverted the water and prevented it from drowning the mine. Hartley and Parkes were hereby for a moment disappointed of executing the scheme they had formed, but they still had it in their power to do it, for they let in water from another place upon the mine they totally drowned their own mine, the consequence was, they drowned that of the trust estate

Gentlemen, it does not rest here, it was of so much consequence to Mr Close and his principals to keep up this level, (for it was the only level they had,) that they deliberated what to do upon it, they at first were advised (and that advice they actually carried into execution) to bring an action against the workmen, who wrought in Mr Smith's ground, not an action for working in ground they had no right to work in, but the action was brought for using their own mines so as to drown their neighbour's they were at last advised that instead of throwing away so much money upon a hazardous experiment at law, it would be better employed in making works to carry the water off. They accordingly dropt their proceedings at law, set to work, erected machines and made pumps to do the business which was formerly more effectually carried on by means of the level of Hartley and Parkes.

Now

Now, Gentlemen, permit me to make a pause here and draw your consideration to the reflections that must naturally arise Was Close ignorant of the rights of this estate? are we, I repeat it, can we be better instructed, is it possible in 1772 to understand the boundaries of an estate sold in 1738, better than the agent of that estate did at that time? was it possible for him to be negligent? What! when the interest of the estate, to which he was agent, called upon him to get what ore he could within this place, when he saw a prospect of profit there, when the interest of his employers absolutely required that they should have dominion over this very ground, though there had not been an ounce of lead raised within the pasture, nay, if there had not been an expectation to tempt any man to make trials there, yet at that time, for the mere object of *dominion* over the ground, it was of infinite consequence for the working their own mines, to assert their right to it, and, had they been conscious of having such right, this would have been their language "This is not your ground, this belongs to Lady Jane Coke, " she only has a right to work, you have no right to work it" That surely would have been a much more easy method of protecting their right than to have been at the expence of 4 or 500l in making a new level to carry on works of their own, which was only necessary because they had no dominion over this part of the estate

Hartley and Parkes discontinued their workings at that place, but revived them in another part of the same ground about a year after. I have stated to you the use of the ground from the year 1743 down to 1748, when this circumstance, so very memorable, happened. From 1753 down to 1762, another period of nine years, there never was a year in which there were not trials and workings in this ground, on the part of Mr Smith's lessees, sometimes they were getting more, sometimes less, but they were continually making trials, and that in view of the trust agents and miners on the other side, what can be said in opposition to this sort of evidence? The Attorney General stated to you that there never were any mines wrought in this place till 1767, when this mine was discovered there might, he said, be some adventurers trying their fortunes, and it was not to be wondered at, if no oppofition was made to them by the truft agents, for in fact, thofe adventurers got nothing

It is impoffible, I am certain, that in a jury of twelve gentlemen of the county of York, there fhould not be fome who have intereft in mines, I fhall to fuch therefore in the firft place obferve, that mens expectations are always full as great as th. reality of any profit turns out And I fancy, gentlemen, that if any of your neighbours were to begin working on your grounds, you would hardly wait to fee whether they made any profit of that working if they were opening mines upon your grounds, I prefume you would think it highly proper to ftop them, without waiting for the chance whether they made any advantage In the next place, there is another anfwer, for whether profitable to the miners or not, it is moft undoubtedly profitable to the Lord, for whoever gains or lofes, if any thing is raifed, it is all clear profit to him.

But it is unneceffary to fearch for other reafons, when the plain fact is a decifive anfwer the mine *was* profitable, there was ore raifed to the amount of near 3000 l the Lord's duty, which was a fixth, amounted to 4 or 500 l which was clear profit to the Lord. Now therefore if 3000 l worth of lead was produced from thefe mines, what becomes of Lord Pomfret's argument? if the owners of the truft eftate were to ftand ftill till profit was made, certainly there was fuch a real advantage as well as profpect of future profit, that it is not poffible to account for their neglect of it But it is faid the parties lived at a diftance, the eftate was under the management of agents who were negligent you, gentlemen, know, that moft mining eftates are, from the nature of the property, under the management of agents The negligence, if any, muft then fall upon Mr Clofe, for as to Lady Jane Coke, tho' fhe might live at a diftance, fhe kept up a conftant correfpondence, and was by no means an inattentive or negligent woman fhe was a very accurate, diftinct, and intelligent perfon, and appears to have been much ufed to bufinefs

Mr.

Mr Close could not be *ignorant*, it is impossible that he should be *negligent*, his own interest would prompt him to be active But then a supposition is adopted, that Close lived in that part of the country, and was connected with the people there, and particularly with Parkes, and thus Mr Close, from a connection with Parkes, (for with Mr Smith he had none) is supposed to have been inattentive to his own interest, for so much as was received from the mines, so much his profit increased in proportion, and he must, according to this position, betray the interest of his employers, at the same time that he gave up his own, this is an improbable supposition, was the fact true of his intimacy with Parkes, but on the contrary it will be proved in point of fact that Close and Parkes were in open enmity, that Close would have been glad to have done Parkes any ill turn he could so that you have every circumstance, his own interest—his duty—the interest of his employers—his resentment against Parke, to induce him to be active and there was but one single circumstance that withheld him from it, which was, the knowledge he had that this place was clearly the property of Mr Smith, that ten thousand people in the country could prove it to be so, that it never had been disputed to be inclosed ground, nor ever would have been, if many circumstances, which I shall state hereafter, had not concurred to make it more worthy to be the prey of those persons who have since extended their views upon it

In 1767, some time after Lord Pomfret's marriage, it happened that the adventurers under Hartley and Parkes, had made trials near Beldy-Hill, which place had, as I have before stated to you, been the subject of continued trials, in none of which they had been fortunate enough to hit upon the vein, but in 1767, it was discovered under promising circumstances, there was great appearance of an immense quantity of ore to be got at that place at the same time the works of the Wharton estate were considerably decayed, the profits of the agents were very small, the profits of the family were exceedingly reduced, I believe very little more was produced than paid the Duchess of Wharton's jointure In that situation, the country talked much of the discovery that had been made by Hartley and

Parkes, and the vast expectation of profit On the other hand, all expectation of profit from the trust mines failing, some very active agents of Lord Pomfret, began to put themselves in motion Persons who were of a very *different stamp* from Mr Close, for had he been agent for the trust estate, he would not, I believe, have interfered Mr Hutchinson, who succeeded Close, and was as well acquainted with the estate as Mr. Close had been, was a man of credit and character in the country, he would not make any forcible entry, nor take violent possession of this mine, although repeatedly urged to it by Lord Pomfret, but rather chose to lose the receivership, than act what he thought (and he thought properly) an unjust and unwarrantable part but there were agents of a very different complexion from either of these. There was a Mr. I'Anson, and a Mr. Metcalf—I will not anticipate what the witnesses will say of Mr. Close's character, it was not only respectable, it was exemplary I need not tell you, gentlemen, any thing of Mr Hutchinson's character, it is very well known to many of you, for the same reason, I will not say any thing of the characters of I'Anson or Metcalf, they too are *universally known* These agents said it was a very good thing to lay claim to this mine I will do Lord Pomfret the justice to say, that I believe he was ignorant of the situation of it his agents told him he had a right, and, if he believed them, it was certainly proper to claim it, accordingly a bill was filed in chancery by Lord Pomfret, claiming this mine. An answer was put in by Mr Smith, stating the circumstances of his right and his Possession by repeated workings in this ground, with the knowledge of the trustees. Upon that answer coming in, application was made by Lord Pomfret to the court of Chancery in 1769, for an injunction to restrain the lessees from working, and upon a full hearing, that injunction was refused.

The court having refused the injunction, Lord Pomfret was advised, (not in Westminster-Hall but in the country) that injunctions in chancery were of very little use—that they were *modern* things, and that in *antient* times, Lords took possession of mines themselves that they made use of their tenants to issue injunctions, so that the injunction

junction which the court of chancery denied him, the noble Lord thought proper to iſſue for himſelf He made an entry, he beat the leſſees workmen from the mine, and began (without the leaſt color of law, but that law, which has been, thank God, many ages aboliſhed in this country) to work the mine, and carried it on to a very conſiderable length. Application was made to the magiſtrates reſpecting this forcible entry, tho' to very little effect, for ſeveral reaſons, which, gentlemen, you know, for thoſe applications made a ſufficient noiſe in the country, and the aſſizes at York have, more than once been acquainted with the circumſtances of that forcible proceeding * Mr Smith, by this means, was compelled to become plaintiff in the court of chancery he filed a bill to be quieted in his poſſeſſion, and for an injunction, ſtating the ſame right as he had done in his anſwer An application was immediately made upon filing the bill, to reſtrain Lord Pomfret from working upon this eſtate, of which he had never any other poſſeſſion, than that which he had taken a month before in a forcible manner. Very unfortunately upon that application, by ſome miſtake of the counſel, (for it could be nothing elſe) it was ſuppoſed that an injunction was ſomething like an attachment, and becauſe the affidavits only mentioned the names of I'Anſon and Metcalf, and did not prove that lord Pomfret *perſonally* had made this entry, the injunction was granted to reſtrain only the *agents*, with a recommendation however at the ſame time to my Lord, as a matter of caution It was ſaid, " It cannot be ſuppoſed that a noble Lord would be guilty of ſuch a conduct, it could only be the unauthorized act of I'Anſon and Metcalf" But this injunction and

* *Lord Pomfret having ſucceeded in his appeal to the Houſe of Lords for a new trial, his agents in the country fancied that they too were above all law, and had a right to do whatever miſchief they pleaſed, accordingly I'Anſon the attorney, and Metcalf the mining agent, went with twenty or thirty of their accomplices to a ſmelt mill of Mr Smith's eight or ten miles from the diſputed ground, and deſtroyed it, for this fact, they were indicted and convicted of a riot at laſt ſummer aſſizes at York, and have ſince been condemned by the court of King's-bench to pay Mr Smith 400l for his damages and coſts*

the

the recommendation were of very little use to Mr Smith, for, the consequence supposed by us, really happened. I'Anson and Metcalf were no longer employed as his Lordship's agents, but a brother of Metcalf's, and a brother attorney of I'Anson's, were immediately employed to work the mine, and the application, which was made just before the long vacation, was of no use to the parties, and I'Anson and Metcalf, under the names of their two substitutes, continued working the mine. Thus a very unusual event happened, a possession, which had continued thirty years without interruption, was taken away by violence That violent possession held for above four months, and very considerable quantities of ore were got in that interval, and converted to the profit of Lord Pomfret

Upon the sitting of the court of chancery in the next term, application was made to the noble Lord who presided with so much ability in that court, for an injunction, and upon Mr. Smith's undertaking to try the question of right, at the next assizes at York, an injunction was issued to restrain all the parties from working beyond a certain district called the *ten meers* Mr Smith without any delay, brought his cause to trial at York, the trial lasted two days, was tried by a jury who had all viewed the place in question, and before a judge of very great abilities, whose absence every person will lament at any time when business comes before this court· during the hearing he exercised the most meritorious patience, the most unexampled diligence, and at that trial, a most extraordinary thing happened, for in the course of two days hearing, in which the closest attention was given, to observe every thing that might convey an hint of the opinion of the judge or jury, neither I, or any of the other counsel, or the parties in the cause, were able to collect the least idea what opinion they had formed upon the question After a full hearing, a verdict was given for Mr. Smith, to the satisfaction of all parties, but the party who lost, which is, I believe generally the case, for the losing party seldom thinks he has justice done him

I shall here, gentlemen, say nothing of the jury who tried that cause, you well know that they are gentlemen of the first character in your

county

county but I cannot pass over one circumstance which is not so generally known, but which does them infinite honor After hearing the cause, they were libelled by every base publication, which could be thrown out in the news-papers,—by hand-bills dispersed about the country,—*by speeches at Market-crosses* What was their conduct on that occasion? they thought, that it was their duty to their country, in respect to the institution of juries, which had been so grossly attacked, to apply to this court, where, regardless of rank and quality, the offender would have met with the censure, which so shameful a conduct richly merited but the moment they heard there was an idea of an application for a new trial, they thought it would be improper in them to appear as parties in the business, they desired I would not move for an information, and to this moment such an outrageous injury to the institution of a jury remains unredressed The verdict of a second jury, will be the best answer to all those infamous libellous publications.

I need not, gentlemen, state to you the variety of proceedings in the court of chancery, the struggles to obtain a new trial of that action,—the opinion of the learned judges,—and particularly of the judge who tried the cause,—the foundation which was urged by Lord Pomfret, as a ground for a new trial nor will I state the proceedings in the House of Lords, upon his Lordship's appeal * I will only say that the Lords *supposed* there was a ground, for what? not for a new trial, but for Lord Pomfret to be at liberty to bring an action, after the appeal Mr Smith expected he would have directly brought such action, and it might have been tried almost immediately, at latest in the course of the ensuing summer. There was not a difficulty in Lord Pomfret's way to prevent his bringing that cause to a trial,

* *It was thought an extraordinary circumstance, that on the very day this appeal was to be heard in the House of Lords, his Majesty should think proper to appoint lord Pomfret a privy counsellor The order for a new trial was carried, on a division, by a majority of only six votes, sixteen being for, and ten against it*

instead

inftead of that, inftead of letting this queftion be tried under precifely the fame circumftances as it was tried before, he deferted the remedy pointed out by the Lords, and profecuted his own unneceffary bill in chancery, he fued out a commiffion for examining witneffes at an enormous expence, not one of whofe depofitions, his advifers muft know, could be read in the court of chancery ✶ This conduct could not anfwer any one purpofe beyond that of vexation and oppreffion, except the wretched purpofe of fixing down witneffes to depofitions, and by the examination on the commiffion, to have an opportunity of ftrengthening a little, the teftimony that might be given

This caufe now comes a fecond time, gentlemen, to be tried, you have heard the evidence which has been given on the part of the plaintiff, and you muft have obferved from the queftions which were put by us, that, excepting in one or two inftances, it is the fame evidence that was produced before, thofe circumftances in which it differs, I fhall have occafion hereafter to comment very particularly upon, and I think I fhall fatisfy the court, that the auxiliary evidence in this bufinefs, (which I will pronounce to be furreptitious evidence,) could have been intended for no other purpofe, but, if poffible, to furprize the confcience of the court, and miflead the counfel, who were unacquainted with the nature of it; but when this evidence is examined, it makes not an Iota of difference between the caufe as it now ftands, and the caufe as it ftood before

I come now, gentlemen, to confider the force of thofe circumftances in Mr Smith's cafe, of which you have not heard any thing till to day, I have not hitherto ftated to you any facts about fences, about depafturing, or any of the circumftances that the witneffes have mentioned But the cafe I have opened to you is irrefiftable, even if we did not produce one of the many witneffes we have to prove the depafturing and the exiftence of antient fences prior to Mr Smith's purchafe.

This, I repeat it again, is an irrefiftable cafe A poffeffion delivered in 1738, and held for thirty years without interruption, and that poffef-

fion

✶ these Depositions were contained in two thousand Sheets of Paper, and the Copy alone cost Mr Smith 100£

ſion ſtrengthened by mining during the whole time. It has been proved that in 1738, this place was delivered to Mr Smith as a part of his purchaſe, each year that he has poſſeſſion confirms the former, and if I had nothing elſe to offer for my client, I ſhould not doubt your verdict upon the mere ſtate of this caſe. I might boldly ſay, " this I purchaſed in 1738" How do you prove it? I prove it by the poſſeſſion taken, I prove it by the poſſeſſion continued, by the teſtimony of all the agents of the truſt eſtate, I prove the ſtrength of that teſtimony by ſtating the ſituations, in which it was their intereſt to oppoſe me if they could, but it was not poſſible to oppoſe me, becauſe it was *then* the ſenſe of all mankind, that this place was part of the eſtate that I purchaſed And, gentlemen, I think no purchaſer of an eſtate could dream he had an infirm title, if his poſſeſſion had remained undiſturbed during a period of thirty years, much leſs would he dream, that the poſſeſſion was to be diſturbed by the repreſentative of the vendor of that eſtate, from whom he received poſſeſſion This gentlemen, is an independant caſe, if there was no other evidence, and I would give them all their boaſted papers, all their teſtimony of their ſheep-hoofs and right of common, and, after that conceſſion, I would with confidence ſay, I am entitled to a verdict If I am not, I do not know upon what ground any poſſeſſor holds his property I am ſure no purchaſer holds it ſecure, if a vendor can at any diſtant period of time ſay, " It is true, I and my agents permitted you to poſſeſs this property; but we have diſcovered we were all ignorant, this matter is better underſtood now than it was when I ſold the eſtate," if this reaſoning ſhall be once admitted, I am certain no man holds his property in ſafety.

You are now, gentlemen, to judge, or more properly to re-judge this caſe, and to determine, whether Mr Smith ſhall enjoy in future, the remains of property which the expence of this diſpute has left him I am ſorry to ſay on the part of Mr Smith, that tho' in this conteſt he has ſucceeded in every ſtep, yet his victories have almoſt undone him Succeſs is ruin to him He was in poſſeſſion, not of a very ample, but of a very eaſy *unincumbered fortune*, he was a man in no *desperate circumstances*, which might induce him, as it has others, to try experiments, this vexatious and expensive contest is not of his own seeking, Lord Pomfret and his advisers have endeavoured to strip him of a great part of his property, and he is now, gentlemen, endeavouring only to preserve what he fairly purchased, against the claims of the representative of the family, under whom he so purchased

Before I come to the second head, or observe upon the evidence given on the part of Lord Pomfret, I must beg leave to fix your attention to the point now to be tried. My learned friend had no interest to state the question in the precise terms that I shall The question that you are now to try, is singly this, "Whether the ground in question *is* part of the commons or wastes of the manor, or not?" that is the single question, and I beg your attention to that, because I am not to argue, nor you to judge, whether it ever *was* part of the commons or wastes I am not obliged to hold the system, that from the creation of the world, down to the present time, this has always been inclosed ground I am to prove what it was at the time of Mr Smith's purchase This is not, gentlemen, a question for antiquarians to decide, it is not a question upon which the court or counsel can give you any assistance, as it is no point of law, but a mere plain matter of fact is this ground part of the inclosure or part of the waste? has Mr Smith a right to hold this piece of ground under a purchase he made thirty years ago? upon this question, the plaintiff undertakes to prove to you, and he must undertake it, that this ground at the time of the purchase was, and he goes further, that it has *since* been considered as waste. Now what it has since been considered, as applied to the plaintiff's case, is certainly of no more consequence than what it was a hundred years ago For the point to which we must apply ourselves is, what this ground was *at the time of the purchase*

LORD

LORD MANSFIELD. What has happened since is only evidence of what it was before You state the question properly, which is, what it was in 1738, *that* is the true question

Mr SOLICITOR GENERAL, It has been constantly possessed since 1738, and lord Pomfret's counsel feel the force of that observation, and to combat that, they have gone into evidence to shew, that since 1738, in the time of modern tenants, this ground has been constantly used as common, now that evidence does not go strictly to the case on either side, and the only reason why I go into the evidence is, because their witnesses have so much overshot the mark, as to destroy the credit of their testimony If you had been told, that after the purchase, a system was formed to acquire the property of the mines in this place, and for that purpose it was necessary to exclude the neighbouring commoners, and consequently, that the use of the pasture had not been much since that time, but that before 1738, the place was common, *that* story would have been at least consistent, but the witnesses chuse to overswear it, they are decisive, they hold the place to have been most visibly and constantly used as common, nay, they carry it to such a degree of improbability, that they suppose Parkes to have made a fence merely for the purpose of fixing the property of the mine, and at the time he made that fence, to have told all the world he was doing it for that avowed purpose, and the witnesses tell you, that the fence was made by Parkes in such a direction, of such a form and figure, that it was notorious to every one who saw it, that it was not a fence for any other purpose, than for the purpose of the mine and they add to that a most palpable absurdity, they suppose that Parkes was attempting to make this inclosed ground not for his own benefit, but for the benefit of somebody when he was dead and gone, and, to add to the absurdity, they prove, that, in order to deceive every person, Mr Parkes was telling all the world the very purpose for which he intended it

My learned friend very prudently passed over all the acts of ownership exercised by Mr Smith's lessees for thirty years below ground He

He has totally dropt all that was done beneath the ſurface, which is infinitely more material than what was done above ground he has confined himſelf to an endeavour to prove the *uſe* of this ground as a common.

I come now, gentlemen, to conſider the proof that has been given for lord Pomfret, which I ſhall range under three heads The uſe and enjoyment of the paſture The name and local deſcription of of the place and the ſtate and condition of the fences belonging to it Under theſe three heads, the whole evidence that has been offered to you on the part of the plaintiff may be comprized Now I will endeavour, under theſe three heads, to give you a ſhort analyſis of what the witneſſes have ſaid, and I will not attend particularly to each witneſs, except where it may be neceſſary to drop a few words upon the perſon's credit.

The firſt is, the *uſe that has been made* of this ground I will make one preliminary obſervation, which I am ſure you will agree is well founded, when you recollect the evidence. The uſe, which the witneſſes ſwear was made of this ground, is as contrary to the ſyſtem they mean to ſupport, as I will ſhew you by our evidence, that it is contrary to truth It is material to obſerve how much they deſtroy the ſyſtem they meant to ſupport. My learned friend called witneſſes to ſhew the practice of this country, with reſpect to the commons There are farms which lie at different diſtances along the river, *Gunnerſide*, *Dykeheads*, *Ivelet*, &c beſides this Crackpot-Hall you have been told, and I believe by your own obſervation you know, that, in theſe commons, it is uſual for the ſeveral tenants in the neighbourhood to have their particular ſheep-hoofs. It was opened to you, that Metcalf, Kearton, Alderſon, and Whitfield, had their reſpective ſheep-hoofs It was alſo opened (with a view to obviate the evidence they knew would be offered on our ſide) that it is uſual for the tenants to dog or hound off their neighbours ſheep when they come upon their ſheep hoofs, that kind of dogging is very different from the hounding of ſheep when they come upon a place where they have no right

to

to come, in the former caſe they run the dog at the ſheep, but it is merely to ſeperate one flock from the other. It was alſo truly ſtated, and the thing ſpeaks it, that the tenants have their ſheep-hoofs on thoſe parts of the waſtes which are moſt contiguous to their farms or ſheep-folds Now, gentlemen, ſuppoſing for a moment, that this place was common, it is apparently the moſt contiguous to Crackpot-Hall farm, it is manifeſt it was ſtocked with Harker's ſheep, and from thence they endeavour to account for the frequent uſe of it by Harker, and for the circumſtance of his dogging off the ſheep of other perſons, of which we have ample and deciſive evidence, this is the ſyſtem laid down, and if the proof had been that the ſheep of other people came there—that they followed the wind and rake, as the witneſſes term it, and came upon this ground, that they were only driven or dogged when they got among Harker's ſheep, that they came there without any moleſtation, and that he never pretended to claim any other right to that ground, but by the cuſtom of the country, as his ſheep-hoof that evidence would have ſupported the opening, and *have borne ſome ſemblance of truth* But you will recollect how far the evidence has gone, not content with proving that caſe, the object of the witneſſes has been to repreſent to you that there were a variety of perſons who had actually a right to ſheep-hoofs on this place, theſe perſons the different witneſſes have ennumerated, and they amount to twelve, they are the tenants of Ivelet, Calverty Houſe, Eaſt and Weſt Stonedales, and other farms which they mentioned.

LORD MANSFIELD I think, to my memory, they have not named ſo many

MR JUSTICE WILLES I have taken down twenty-three

MR SOLICITOR GENERAL I believe, ſir, you are more correct than I, but when I came to twelve, I ſtopt, for that number is juſt as good for my argument as twenty-three.

LORD

LORD MANSFIELD. They ſpeak to the ſheep-hoofs of different tenants at different times, eſpecially while Harker and Metcalfe were tenants

MR. SOLICITOR GENERAL. I have taken twelve of them all in *one* period I dare ſay your lordſhip's notes are very correct, but take it either in the time of Harker, or of Metcalfe, and examine the witneſſes, you will find they give you no leſs than twelve neighbouring tenants at one and the ſame time, who not only drove their ſheep there, but all had their ſheep-hoof upon the ſpot I pointed the queſtions particularly, and the witneſſes, on their preſent examination, went a great deal farther than upon the former trial. The reaſon is obvious, if they had only ſaid, they ſaw ſheep go there, and ſaw them driven off, whether by the owner or any one elſe, the obſervation would have been the ſame as on the former trial, but this certainly is not evidence of a common right Inſtead, therefore, of proving they ſaw the tenants take their ſheep away from the place, they ſwear they ſaw them put them on, and they have raiſed themſelves to the idea, that it was *neceſſary* to prove that the different people, who they ſuppoſed to have the promiſcuous uſe of this ground, had actually their ſheep-hoofs upon it nor is that all, for they all venture to be poſitive they never ſaw Harker drive any ſheep from it You will obſerve, that when they talk of his driving or hounding, they ſay, he drove his neighbours ſheep *out* of Beldy Hill Cow Paſture into the place in queſtion, and they ſay, that he drove his own ſheep alſo I do not in the leaſt queſtion it, for no doubt he would drive his own ſheep if they came out of this paſture into the hay ground Now, gentlemen, whether the ground in queſtion was common, or not, if it is but ſuppoſed to be Harker's ſheep-hoof, if Harker is but ſuppoſed to have a right to have his ſheep there, is it not amazing, that ſcarce one of Lord Pomfret's witneſſes could be brought to ſpeak diſtinctly that they ever had ſeen Harker's ſheep on the ſpot?

LORD MANSFIELD Several have

MR.

Mr Solicitor General. Yes, my lord, but then they ſay it was by chance, and as a caſual thing, none ſpoke of his having his ſheep-hoof there. If Harker's ſheep went there only in right of his ſheep-hoof, yet it is incredible that no one ever ſaw him drive off his neighbour's ſheep. It was opened to you, and admitted as a fact, that he did ſo, and yet these witneſſes who would have it ſuppoſed they very frequently obſerved this place, and had great reaſon to know it, do not allow that Harker ever hoofed his ſheep there, or that he ever drove off those of his neighbours. This evidence goes ſo far beyond the mark, that it deſtroys all credit to their teſtimony.

Beſides, ſuppoſing the number of perſons who had ſheep-hoofs upon this place to be only twelve, yet when they come to compute the ſtock belonging to theſe ſeveral tenants, they give to ſome fourſcore, to others five and ſix ſcore, add them together, you will find that above *one thouſand ſheep*, at a moderate computation, muſt have been hoofed upon it. You, gentlemen, have ſeen the place, and therefore I need ſay little about it, it contains, 'tis true, two hundred and forty acres, but I am told it is the moſt barren ſpot in the kingdom, and if it had not been for the expectation below ground, it would not have been thought worth contending for. The ground, I am told by a good judge of land, is not worth more than nine-pence an acre, and I am likewiſe told, that the utmoſt quantity of ſheep that could be ſtocked upon it is five or ſix ſcore. As you have ſeen it, you are competent judges whether it is poſſible that the quantity of ſheep they have ſworn to, could be depaſtured upon this place, even ſuppoſing it common: their account ſurpaſſes all belief, nor can it be conceived why all the ſheep of the country ſhould have been ſo particularly fond of this ſpot, for the witneſſes have in fact collected them all there. That they might have ſtrayed there, may be very natural, but that there ſhould be any inducement to the ſheep to have taken that courſe, I cannot conceive.—Gentlemen, you will obſerve, that out of the number of witneſſes (and they are not wanting in *number*) they have called only two perſons who belonged to the family of any of the four ſucceſſive tenants of the farm, *Jane Moore* and *John*

Harker

Harker. All the connection that Jane Moore had with the family of Harker was, that ſhe lived there the winter half year The other witneſs, John Harker, is indeed a nephew of old Simon Harker, but he was not a hired ſervant with him, and all the account that he gives of his connection with the place, is, that he once ſtaid ſix weeks on a viſit with his uncle, when young Theſe are the only two perſons they have called belonging to the families of the ſeveral tenants. Gentlemen, we ſhall produce on the other ſide ſeven or eight perſons of the family of each of thoſe tenants, ſome of great age from the family of Harker, ſome of very advanced years from the families of Metcalfe and Scot: they will give you an account of the uſe thoſe tenants ſucceſſively made of this paſture I will not now anticipate that evidence, I only hint it to ſet in contraſt the credit due to the account given by the one and the other.

It is remarkable, one of their witneſſes, Simon Broderick, gives evidence of his own ſheep going on this paſture undiſturbed by Harker, and to ſhew you with how little accuracy their ideas are formed of it, he tells you at the ſame time, that his ſheep had no right to go there, for he did not live within the manor, nay, even expreſly ſtated, that he lived out of the manor.

MR. JUSTICE WILLES He belonged to a neighbouring manor

MR SOLICITOR GENERAL His ſheep were bought *within* the manor, but I apprehend the ſheep do not from that circumſtance acquire any birth-right to live upon the manor, when their owner had no right and yet this man, in juſt the ſame terms as the reſt, talked of his ſheep going undiſturbed on this ground as a matter of right This is an incredible circumſtance, for, whether it was common or not, nay admit it to be common, this man's ſheep had no right to go there, they were much more likely to go there if it was the private property of Harker, than if it was the property of all the tenants of the manor, becauſe, as a collective body, they would be more vigilant about their right than any ſingle perſon. As to many of the other

other witnesses, you, gentlemen, must have observed the little degree of accuracy with which they speak. I do not wonder at it; I only wonder that being so little accurate, they dare to be so positive. I will give you one instance *of their extreme inaccuracy* when they descend to facts. James Hawkins, one of their witnesses, swears, that Edmund Coates depastured his horses on this place as on a common. Now I am amazed, gentlemen, at their venturing to repeat this circumstance, as the evidence on both sides is known; for we proved at York, and shall prove again, that this very Edmund Coates's cattle depastured there, and well they might, for he paid Harker for their feeding. We have Coates himself to prove the positive fact, and that goes much farther than any evidence of opinion.

Lord Pomfret's witnesses are not agreed in fixing, with precision, the season of the year when they saw the cattle feeding; neither are they accurate in fixing the precise spot on which they fed. As to their not fixing the season of the year, the effect of that observation I am sure you anticipate; but it may be proper just to mention, that it will appear to you in evidence, that this pasture was herded and hounded with diligence in the summer, in the winter no persons gave themselves any trouble about it, for a plain reason; it was in summer a benefit to have the grass, but in winter the pasture and the adjoining wastes were so much alike, that it was not worth while to employ a person to look after it. On this head of evidence I would observe, that the witnesses are in general extremely inaccurate; that, when they descend to particular circumstances, you will find those circumstances totally contradicted or explained away; that the witnesses, excepting the two I have mentioned, are no ways connected with the families of any of the tenants of the farm, and, in general, that they have prodigiously overdone the matter, and proved a great deal too much to deserve any credit.

There are two of the plaintiff's witnesses I must take a little notice of, Liddell and Whitfield; Liddell speaks to a circumstance, that if I understand his testimony *one* way, there is certainly very little in it, and it may be true, for I am willing to suppose, wherever it is possible for me to do it, that the witnesses have not wilfully adopted a story that has no foundation or color whatever In many circumstances they swear falsely, without swearing wickedly, they form systems to themselves, they push their opinions farther than they ought, and, at a great distance of time, they misapply things and circumstances, and, though they swear wrong, yet it is not always with an intention to impose a falshood! The account Liddell has given, is, that Metcalfe (who was tenant at Crackpot Hall after Simon Harker) claimed this place, with the common beyond it, as far as the northern boundary of the manor extended (which is above two miles) for his sheep-hoof, that he, Liddel, then tenant at East-stonsdale, insisted that his sheep-hoof was on that part of the common adjoining his farm on both sides the Beck, extending, on the east side, into the ground in question, which claim interfering with Metcalfe's sheep-hoof, they had a dispute about it, which, he says, was referred to Wilson, Mr Smith's steward, who said, that Liddell had as much right on the east side of the Beck as Metcalfe Now, gentlemen, you will recollect, Liddell, when pressed on his cross examination, told you, that though a few of his sheep might go on the place in question, yet the bulk of his sheep usually fed in the north part of the wastes The other witness, Whitfield, affects to be much more pointed and decisive than Liddell, and therefore I must beg you, gentlemen, to attend very particularly to his evidence He does not speak of the dispute as a matter of doubt, he swears positively the dispute was about feeding upon the ground in question, and as he was exact as to the place, I wished to bring him exact as to the time in which the dispute happened He swears that it was the very next year after Harker quitted Crackpot Hall, which, it is admitted on both sides, was in 1740 He swears the matter was referred to Mr. Wilson, who called in the assistance of Harker, and that Wilson determined that Liddell had an equal right with Whitfield, to have his sheep-hoof upon the ground in question Now, gentlemen, having fixed him as to place and time, I will prove to you, beyond a possibility of doubt, that the whole must be an absolute fiction, and I am, am really concerned that the old man has been ſo very particular, becauſe it is impoſſible for me to ſave the conſcience of the witneſs, by ſuppoſing a confuſion in his ideas The fact was, and it will be proved beyond a doubt, that Wilſon was not appointed ſteward till the latter end of 1741, he never acted as ſuch, or ever went into that part of the country till the ſummer of 1742, ſo that it was impoſſible for any reference to be made to Wilſon till above a year after the time which Whitfield has fixed as the date of that reference This very circumſtance, gentlemen, would overturn the whole of Whitfield's evidence, even if I had nothing to contradict it, but, gentlemen, when I come to produce Mr Wilſon, the very man to whom this reference is ſuppoſed to have been made, he poſitively and directly denies he ever heard of the exiſtence of ſuch a diſpute, or that any ſuch reference was made to him by Whitfield or Liddell

I ſhall here cloſe my obſervations upon the plaintiff's witneſſes, with reſpect to the right claimed by the neighbouring tenants to ſheep-hoofs on the ground in queſtion, this evidence you will ſee abundant reaſon to pay not the leaſt credit to, and, having overturned that evidence, I will now juſt give you a view of our evidence of the actual *uſe and enjoyment* of this place, by Mr Smith's tenants, as part of Crackpot Hill farm

I ſhall call ſeven or eight witneſſes of the family of Harker, ſome of whom will ſpeak to facts ſo far back as the year 1710, and *that* from certain knowledge, they will prove that Harker (who was fifty years tenant of this farm) uſed this paſture as his ſeparate property, that he kept his own ſheep there, that he drove off thoſe of every other perſon, that he not only drove them off, but drove them off with an illegal violence, in ſhort, that ſo far from there being no inſtance of his heading his own, and driving off thoſe of others, the inſtances were frequent and repeated, many of them very outrageous ones, that the tenants of the ſurrounding farms have at times had occaſion to complain of Harker's ſeverity, and they went ſo far as to call a meeting for the purpoſe of conſulting whether they ſhould not

bring

bring an action against Harker for not repairing his fences, and for hounding their sheep so violently.

They will also prove Harker's agisting not only his own cattle on the spot, but his taking in the cattle of others for hire they will prove the existence of fences round the place long before the purchase, that Harker repaired them, in a slovenly manner indeed, but still that they were repaired they will prove the same facts in the time of Metcalfe, the succeeding tenant, that he had the like enjoyment of it as Harker had, we shall likewise prove that Scot, the tenant that succeeded Metcalfe, took this very pasture as part of his bargain, that he understood it to be part of the farm, and that while he was tenant, he enjoyed it as such we shall prove by the family, by the neighbours on all hands, that it has been acknowledged to be the property of Harker, of Metcalfe, and of Scot successively, that the sheep of the surrounding tenants sometimes came there, sometimes the parties were neighbourly, sometimes not, but that Harker, in particular, was extremely cross and sturdy in asserting his right to this place This, gentlemen, is the evidence we shall produce, with regard to the use of the pasture, and this evidence will infinitely counterbalance any thing that has been offered on the other side

I next come to the proof of the *name and local description of the place* Their witnesses call it *Hall Moor*, or *Hall Edge*, we call it *Hall Pasture*, or *Out Pasture* Had their witnesses proved only affirmatively that it was called by the names of Hall Edge and Hall Moor, that evidence would have been of little consequence, for I have no doubt of its having different names given it by different persons, according to their different situations or residence People who live contiguous to that part of a country which strikes their eye, are apt to call the place by that name In this pasture there are places called by different names, there is Swinnergill Edge, Hall Edge, and Cross Green Edge, so that Hall Edge is a known appellation, it does not mean the whole, only a part, but may very often be used for the whole Hall Moor was another term used by the witnesses

I observed

I obferved the plaintiff's council, in the opening, fell into a miftake, it was taken for granted, that *moor* and *wafte* were fynonymous terms, certainly they are not fo, there are many places under the denomination of moor, that are not commons or waftes, Hall Moor does not imply that the place fo called is a common your own knowledge, gentlemen, will fatisfy you that there are many places in the county that are called moors of different denominations, that have, as far as memory can extend, been inclofed and ufed as private property, but ground that is of a moorifh quality will be frequently called by the appellation of *moor*

As to the *name*, that would not have much deferved an obfervation, if the witneffes had only fpoken to this place being known by the name of Hall Moor, and Hall Edge, but they have all fworn negatively, that they never knew it called by the name of Crackpot Out Pafture, or Hall Pafture, till this difpute arofe But there is one circumftance I muft beg your attention to, when feveral of the witneffes were fpeaking of Harker's driving cattle out of a particular piece of ground, part of the farm, pleafe to attend to the name they all ufe, they univerfally called it the *In Pafture*, he hounded his neighbours fheep out of his *In Pafture* upon the place in queftion Now was there an *In Pafture* and not an Out Pafture upon this farm? They are all familiar with the term *In Pafture*, but totally ignorant of that of the *Out Pafture*

MR JUSTICE WILLES I do not remember that circumftance

MR SOLICITOR GENERAL William Clofe faid, if they came into the *In Pafture*, they were dogged out upon the place in queftion

JURY Yes, he did fay fo

MR SOLICITOR GENERAL And feveral more of the witneffes. But, gentlemen, this defcription of Crackpot Hall Out Pafture is far from being a new invention, it was the name ufed by Harker, and all the fucceeding tenants, and indeed nothing could be fo abfurd as

to

to suppose that this name was first given to it in 1767 it is directly the reverse, for when Parkes took a lease in 1743, it is in that very lease expressly called Crackpot Hall Out Pasture, but then it was urged, this name was given it with a view to the mines But, gentlemen, would any one be so ridiculous to take a lease of a place under a false description, in order for it to assume that name at the end of thirty years? it is incredible When people take a lease they take it by a description agreeable to truth and to the common language used If I take a lease of any man, certainly neither he nor I should call *Black-acre* White acre, when we were wanting to ascertain what I took, and he lett, but it does not rest only upon that, the witnesses will give you an account of the Hall Pasture, or Out Pasture, being the well known name of the place, and they distinguish the In Pasture from the Out Pasture, in the same manner that some of the plaintiff's own witnesses have done. And is it credible that there should be an In Pasture and not an Out Pasture? Before I dismiss this head, give me leave to make one observation, arising from the indefinite description of Hall Moor, their witnesses have been pleased to call the whole extent of ground, northward of the farm, (which is some miles) Hall Moor, they do not stop short at what we call the northern boundary of the place in question, and fix its limits there, when therefore they speak of seeing sheep turned on, and feeding upon Hall Moor, and not being driven off, I say, when they do not particularize the place, and bring it to a specific spot, I can very easily, without imputing direct perjury to them, account for their swearing in that manner. They are misled by the Hall Moor's extending farther north, for it is certainly true, that sheep have been put upon, have been depastured, and have not been drove off Hall Moor but when they apply their evidence of such facts to the place in question, that evidence is as certainly false This confusion is easily brought about by a little *management*, the applying the name Hall Moor to two different places, misleads the witnesses.

I shall next consider the *state and condition of the fences* You, gentlemen, can here judge yourselves of the credit that is to be given

to

to the witnesses, when they tell you that there is not so much as a *foundation of a fence*, when the *gentleman-surveyor* (who was examined) comes to tell you of what was or was not to be observed of the existence of a fence, or the traces or foundations of walls and gutters, which, he says, he endeavoured to trace with his feet, there you certainly will not give more credit to that *gentleman's* nice feeling of his toes (even with the assistance of Mr Chaytor) than you will to your own eyes

Mr Chaytor Sir, you made use of my name.

Mr Solicitor Yes, sir, I did, and shall make much more use of it before I have done —You, gentlemen, will give, I say, much more credit to what you yourselves have observed, than to any thing the witnesses can tell you, as to the present state and condition of the fences, it is therefore to no purpose to call witnesses to prove what either was or ought to have been shewn to you upon the view the witness has spoken of gutters, some of you, gentlemen, said, that you did not remember any such as that witness described If so, give me leave to say, that the conduct of the shewers for Lord Pomfret, on the view, was extremely unfair, if they did not shew you these gutters, when they intended to make use of them in evidence You either saw this place, or you did not, if you was carried to the place, and yet was not shewn the whole of it when you was there, it is an unfair conduct, they ought to have shewn you all the bearings, points, and directions of the place, to leave it to your own eyes, and not to the eyes of people that are to give evidence here, so that whether you was shewn these gutters, or not, is immaterial to my argument, in one case, if you have seen them, the evidence will not gain credit, in the other, if you was not shewn them, you will not believe the evidence so unfairly introduced

I will not trouble you with any evidence as to the *present* state of the fences, if the witnesses do speak to it, it will be from their own disposition to tell their own story, but I will not take up your time in

ask ng

aſking them about the ſtate and condition of fences that you have actually ſeen

It is very ſingular that the other ſide has only examined as to the ſtate and condition of the *northern fence* of the paſture, they have examined nothing about the *eaſtern* or *weſtern* parts of the fence Their queſtions have all been, What have you ſeen on the north ſide, from the water rail to a place in Swinnergill called Hind Hole? and, I take it for granted, by their ſilence upon that head, that there is a good fence on the eaſt and weſt ſides, natural indeed in ſome places, but in others artificial. And, gentlemen, if I find three ſides of a field actually incloſed, I am juſtified in ſuppoſing the fourth ſide muſt have been, or was intended to be incloſed, becauſe I cannot conceive that any perſon would have erected three ſides of a fence for no purpoſe at all, and the exiſtence of fences on the eaſt and weſt is juſt as material to the purpoſe of this queſtion, and to Mr Smith's title, as the exiſtence of a fence on the north ſide of the paſture, and yet the plaintiff has confined his evidence merely to this, whether there was any fence on the north ſide.

I am inſtructed that you have ſeen the traces of a fence, not only on the eaſt and weſt ſides of the paſture, but alſo the traces of a fence on the north ſide, that there are ſtone walls built where the ſcars or rocks did not make a natural fence, that whenever the nature of the ground did not permit a wall to be made, there was a ſod fence, with a gutter on each ſide, and you muſt have remarked that this is not modern work, or like thoſe walls that are found in other places upon the waſtes, for here are the regular veſtiges of a wall at each angle, and there are in other places, if any perſon would take the pains (which the ſurveyor was too much a *fine gentleman* to take) to turn up the ſoil, they would find the regular and continued foundations of a wall and fence This, gentlemen, I am inſtructed is the caſe, you beſt know whether it is fact.

The

The queſtion is not what the fences now are, but what they were in former times: you are told, indeed, by all the plaintiff's witneſſes that there are bits of old walls, but that they remember a certain period when there was nothing like a fence. No one, I believe, will ſuppoſe that we are talking of a fence ſufficient to keep out Yorkſhire ſheep, the fence even of the In Paſture was not ſufficient for that purpoſe; but it will be proved that there was a fence ſufficient to turn cattle, in which there were driving gaps, and thirls for ſheep to go through. But then Lord Pomfret contends, that this fence was firſt erected about the year 1746, and to prove that, witneſſes are called in to account for the fences you have ſeen, and they boldly ſwear, that Parke made this fence in 1746, and that none exiſted before that period. The firſt of theſe witneſſes is Whitfield, on whoſe evidence, on another occaſion, I have remarked, he ſays, he ſpoke to Parkes's workmen while they were erecting this fence, and directed them to deſiſt from making, what? why merely, according to his account, from making a gutter two feet broad and one foot deep: what reaſon did he give? leſt he ſhould loſe his lambs in it. Obſerve the abſurdity of the reaſon; for no man could be ever apprehenſive of loſing his lambs in a gutter of that ſize, and yet he is poſitive in his evidence. They have produced another witneſs, one Wilſon, a chairman; you, gentlemen, obſerved in what manner he gave his teſtimony: he ſwears boldly, that he was employed by Parkes to make the fence in 1746; that he worked there; and he remembers the time particularly, becauſe he had a quarrel with Edward Smallman, a fellow workman, that they ſought, and he hurt his knee: he tells a ſtory, that Parkes ſaid, while the fence was making, that he believed they would remember it when he was dead and gone, and that he, Wilſon, replied, he ſhould remember his knee alſo. This is the evidence they have brought to prove that theſe fences were made by Parkes in 1746 with a view to the mines. We have, in contradiction to this, the moſt direct, flat, and deciſive anſwer, they know we have; and I am therefore aſtoniſhed they ſhould riſque the production of that fellow. Our anſwer ſo fully overturns his evidence, that it is, in fact, a contradiction to the whole of their caſe.

In the firft place, as to this Wilfon, he is a new acquifition, found in the ftreets of London fince the laft trial, for he was not produced at York, and what he has fworn, I boldly affert, is an abfolute falfehood, that he ever worked in the place, is an abfolute falfehood, that he ever had a difpute with Smallman, is directly falfe, that he was even in the country at the time he fwears to the fact, is abfolutely falfe, the whole of the ftory is merely an invention of the witnefs, without any other foundation or colour, than this, that he is the fon of one Wilfon, who actually was employed to repair this fence, and the brother of one Wilfon, who alfo worked at it It you recollect, gentlemen, he was by accident interrupted fome time in the courfe of of his examination, when the examination was refumed, he had loft himfelf, he could not take up the ftory where he left off he told the counfel, " I muft begin at the beginning again " The production of this man is the moft outrageous infult to juftice, for there is not a fyllable of truth in his evidence to contradict him, I fhall call his father, his brother, I fhall call Edward Smallman, and I fhall call Pratt, they were all employed at the repair of thefe fences in 1746 I am forry to fay the father will be obliged to give you but a bad account of his fon, and both father and brother, and Smallman and Pratt, pofitively fwear, that this man never was employed about the fences, nay more, that he had actually left the country a confiderable time before, and was, at the very time he fwears to, a chairman in London.

Lord Mansfield Was this witnefs examined under the commiffion?

Mr Solicitor General. He was.

Lord Mansfield. I afk, becaufe of your being fo prepared to anfwer him.

Mr. Solicitor General. We had at York the father, the fon, and Smallman and Pratt, they knew we were in poffeffion of thefe witneffes, witnesses, and yet the cause is so desperate, that they risque bringing even such a fellow as this, whose testimony they knew must be contradicted, it is bold! but where a case is desperate, people must run risques

The fact, as to the repair of the fences, is this, and to support that fact you will find how immensely strong the proof is in favour of Mr Smith In the first place, Parkes neither made nor even ever repaired the fence, nay, had not so much as the least concern with the making or repairing of it.

Simon Harker, when in possession, before Mr Smith's purchase, had made application to the agents of the Duke of Wharton to have this fence repaired, those agents pressed Harker to repair it himself, and give as a reason, that the expence of herding was more than the expence of repairing would be no, said he, I will not repair it, it will cost me too much, but I will repair it if you will allow me a year's rent This the duke's agents declined to do, but after the purchase, Metcalfe, the succeeding tenant, in 1746, desired to have the fence repaired, he applied to Wilson, Mr Smith's steward, to have the fence repaired, he agreed to do it, and, without any connection with Parkes, employed Wilson, the father of the chairman, to do the stone work Wilson employed his other son, and Smallman and Pratt, he contracted for it at a shilling a rood for labour only, Smallman and Pratt were employed to do the sod fence, they worked by measure, Wilson, the steward, paid the workmen their bills, and charged it to Mr Smith's account, and we will prove to you the sums allowed in those accounts This, gentlemen, is the history of the repairing the fences, in contradiction to the evidence they have boldly and impudently produced on the other side, and give me leave to add that every one of our witnesses, who will prove this case, are men of good credit, character and condition, they will swear, that in repairing the fences, they followed the line of the old fence, that such line was, extremely visible to them, that they regularly took that as their course and direction, that they were directed to go by it, and that they did not deviate an inch from it, nor make any fence where there was no fence before. I need not tell the jury, nor, in this stage of the cause, need I tell your lordship, that from the nature of the ground, in some places, and from the weather, frequent accidents must happen to a sod fence, that wet ground will often vary, the workmen therefore, to be certain of their line, took along with them old Simon Harker, who pointed out to them the course of this fence where it was obscure by the accidents I have mentioned, and I am told that severe weather will very much alter the appearance of these fences, especially when frost holds in Our witnesses are all positive (and they give good reason for it), that they followed the line of the old fence, and that it was not a new work, but the foundation and remains of the ancient fence were extremely visible to any man who would chuse to see it, and some of the workmen will particularly tell you, that, in making the sod fence, they found buried under ground the old posts that had manifestly served for gate posts to catch the gate, to let out and drive in cattle into this pasture, and we shall prove, that in 1746, the fences were, previous to the repair, in much better condition than at present.

This, gentlemen, is a sketch of the evidence I shall lay before you as to the fence of the pasture, and I venture to state this evidence confidently, it has already been given at York, and had there its due weight. It is of immense consequence in this cause, to shew the existence of the fence prior to the purchase, and the use and enjoyment of the ground will weigh against a thousand witnesses, which cannot be answered by saying, that there are traces of fences on other parts of the moor of a similar nature.

Besides this, gentlemen, if I am not much mistaken, the witnesses will give you (for they have given it already at York) an account of other appearances in this ground, in ancient times this pasture was not all one single inclosure, there were within it two Closes, that are now lying open, called Gill closes, in these places there are the remains of an house and out-buildings, the ruins of which, the witnesses

nesses will tell you, are visible to this day, that there are the traces of small inclosures round the house and buildings, which plainly indicate that some person had dwelt there, tradition says, and the old witnesses will give you an account of it, that in ancient times this inclosure was made for the Lord's deer, and the old people said the persons that kept the Lord's deer lived in that house, this is but tradition, but I think tradition will be as good evidence as the old papers, produced with so much exultation the other night by Mr Chaytor

LORD MANSFIELD. Are the High Gill Closes common?

MR SOLICITOR GENERAL There are High Gill Closes and Low Gill Closes The Low Gill Closes are those I speak of, they were formerly taken out of this pasture, and are part of the two hundred and forty Acres.

LORD MANSFIELD The High Gill Closes are common.

MR SOLICITOR GENERAL Yes I am now furnished, (no thanks however to Mr Chaytor) with an additional piece of evidence with regard to the northern fence of the pasture; for, if I am not much mistaken, one of the papers produced by him the other night, (*how* introduced I shall reserve for another consideration) contains evidence of *building* a wall which cannot apply to any other than the northern boundary of the pasture, and my reason for saying so, is this, that paper is, if I did not mistake, later in point of date than the other, (I speak from memory), I think it is a year after, the agreement is the last of the two, if so, then the other paper plainly and satisfactorily points out the closes of which the farm then consisted, and it points them out as *closes*, *ergo* they were manifestly *inclosed* in 1635, then in the next year 1636, there is an agreement, that the Lord shall *build* a wall on the upper side of the ground, from Stonesdale Beck to Swinnergill Beck now if your lordship and the jury will only take the trouble of looking, for the purpose of the observation, upon the

map

map, it is most manifest, that, if a man knew what he was describing, this could never be the description of the wall, which they now contend to be the northern boundary of the farm In the first place, it is not the upper side of the ground, it does not go in a line from Beck to Beck, it would be just as absurd in language to say, that it is a streight line from hence to St James's by Charing-cross, as to say this goes in a direct line from Swinnergill Beck to Stonesdale Beck, for it goes in a line from Swinnergill to a place called the Smithy, then turns north a great way, and after that takes a western direction and comes down to Stonesdale Beck Now no man that was treating about building a wall in the course and direction contended for by the other side would say, "I'll build you a wall on the upper side this ground from Swinergill Beck to Stonesdale Beck," (which implies in itself that they are two places in a direct line from each other), no, he would say, "I will build you a wall from Swinnergill to the Smithy, from thence to such a place northward, and so to Stonesdale Beck" It is remarkable that there are no less than three lines in the course of that fence, which is supposed to surround all the parcels of land that are allowed to be the ancient inclosures of the farm Now, gentlemen, you see by the map the effect of the observation But it does not rest here only, the Lord is agreeing with his own tenant that he will build him a wall, their supposition is, that it was to be a stone wall to fence in all his different closes towards the north I believe I need not tell you, gentlemen, that there could be no other fences there at that time than a dry stone wall. No one will imagine that in 1636, there could be good hawthorn hedges The man treating with his own tenant, says to him, not that he will *repair* the fences, but that he will *build* a stone wall from Beck to Beck, one should naturally suppose, that these two points were to be approached in a streight line, no, say they, when the Lord says to his hind, "I'll build you a stone wall from Beck to Beck," he means, I will build you a stone wall on the line of all the old inclosures, according to the waving directions of these inclosures

MR JUSTICE WILLES What is meant by the fire-house?

MR. WAL-

Mr. Wallace It means a dwelling-house for the hind to live in, or an house with a chimney in it

Lord Mansfield. You are, Mr Solicitor, very correct in the paper, as you state it I should be glad to have the topography taken, it may be material; I should be glad to know whether that course tallies with either of the walls

Mr Solicitor General That tallies undoubtedly with what we call the boundary, but the wall they contend for, manifestly does not go in a line from Beck to Beck.

Lord Mansfield Do the two Becks go so low as to go to the east and west points of that wall?

Mr Attorney General The Becks both fall into the Swale.

Mr Solicitor General. But your lordship sees, that the wall inclosing cross greens in the map runs a great way north The point between the Beck and the Swale does not make an angle in the farm, therefore the wall that they assign for our boundary, manifestly does not go from Beck to Beck, for from the Smithy it takes a northern direction to the top of Cross Greens, and then goes towards the Beck, it is, I am told, near a mile from the angle at which the fence quits that western direction and goes due north. It certainly is not the language of a man, if he understands what he speaks, to say, "I will build a stone wall from Beck to Beck," unless he means a wall which it is possible to carry in a direct line if it is to be understood that the Lord was to build a stone wall, then it is manifest, there could be no wall on the upper side of the ground before, and, if a wall was built in consequence of this agreement, it cannot correspond with any other than the wall we contend to be the northern boundary it cannot apply to the wall they contend for, because *that* existed at the very date of the agreement itself, and therefore the expression would

would have been, "I will *repair*," not *build* a wall from Beck to Beck

Gentlemen, I have gone through the three several heads under which I purposed to range the evidence, and stated to you my observations upon it, I shall now proceed to take notice of the plaintiff's *auxiliary evidence*, which has certainly been fabricated since the trial at York. They knew the strength of our evidence as to the enjoyment of this pasture as part of the farm, without any claim or interruption since the purchase, they thought it prudent therefore to *procure* some evidence that would directly combat our proof, and the purport of that evidence is this, that for several years after Mr Smith's purchase, there were some persons who actually worked, what they call waste bargains, on the west side of Swinnergill Beck, within the ground in question, that such bargains were taken of the agents of the trust estate, that they paid a duty to such trust agents on account of the ore they got, that these bargains were worked openly, and with the knowledge of the tenants of the farm, who never interrupted or molested them in their workings To prove this story, they have produced one Askin, a man who ran away from the country near thirty years ago, he swears, that in 1739, he took a waste bargain of the trust agents on the west of Swinnergill, in the ground in question. That he and three others, whom he names, worked there for a considerable time, that they worked by means of a water race which flowed from above Hind Hole, in the place in dispute, which enabled them to wash or buddle the waste ore,—that, when he quitted the country, he sold his bargain to Robinson and Miller, who continued working on the spot for some years after

Now, gentlemen, for a moment, I might admit the fact they have *attempted* to prove, and yet deny the conclusion they would draw from it When Mr Smith purchased, there were subsisting bargains, those were excepted in the conveyance to Mr Smith, this might have been one of them —In those waste bargains the party does not dig for ore, he only takes the refuse that has been left on the surface [illegible] by the former workers of the mines, *that* refuse they wash and buddle, and are paid by the parties, or whom the bargains are taken, such a certain sum of money for each horse-load or bing of ore they get from such refuse.

But gentlemen, I have no occasion to explain their evidence by supposing this a subsisting bargain at the time of the purchase, when I have a better answer to make, viz. the whole of the story is a *direct falsehood*, and I am able to prove it so by irresistible evidence. It will be proved to you, that the waste bargain taken and worked by Askin and the people under him, was on the *east* side of Swinnergill Beck, within the *trust liberties*, we shall not only prove that fact, but also, that they never worked on the *west* side of the Beck, we shall go further, and prove it impossible that it could have been on Mr Smith's ground, for we shall prove, that in 1739, there was no waste left by the former miners on that side of the Beck that was capable of producing an ounce of ore, and we shall prove there was waste on the *east* side of the Beck.—We shall prove that the very water race, which has been so confidently sworn to, and described to have been made in Mr Smith's ground to enable them to wash and buddle, was actually on the *east* side of the Beck *within the wastes of the manor*, at a place called the Middle Tongue.—We shall prove this, not only by the evidence of Mr Elliot and Mr. Stoddart, the trust agents, and many others, but also by one William Clarkson, who actually worked with Askin at this bargain at the time,—we shall, to close the whole, produce the accounts of Mr Close, the receiver of the trust estate, which fix beyond a doubt Askin's, Robinson's, and Miller's working to have been on the wastes of the manor at a considerable distance from this pasture.—I should not have thought it necessary to have gone into evidence to contradict this proof, but I shall do it to convince you, that in every step they have taken to get out of the Difficulties this cause was attended with the last time, instead of extricating themselves, they have plunged up to the neck in falsehood, a conduct that is even a greater discredit to those that *procured* such evidence, than to the very witnesses themſelves As to Aſkin, I can have great charity for him, he lives at an inn in Staffordſhire, and, at the diſtance of near thirty years, he is brought and ſhewn the ſpot, he is taken where they pleaſe to carry him, and then it is the eaſieſt thing in the world, for artful agents (who ſtick at nothing) to make a man believe what they would have him believe

Gentlemen, I have now done with the obſervations on the evidence on the part of the plaintiff, on the part of the defendant, I began with opening to you a caſe independant of any thing the plaintiff's witneſſes either had or could ſwear, I ſhall proceed in that order, and ſhall call witneſſes to ſhew to you the workings of Hartley and Parkes as leſſees of Mr Smith, from the time of his purchaſe, I will prove to you, that they entered in 1743, that they then began and continued thoſe workings down to the commencement of the preſent diſpute in 1767, without the leaſt interruption on the part of the truſt agents, I will prove, that the truſt agents were acquainted with the condition of the eſtate, that they were men of honeſty, vigilance and attention I will ſhew you that it was their intereſt to attend to theſe workings, that it was even the intereſt of their paſſions to ſupport the right of their principals. I will ſhew you that they were called upon every day to aſſert thoſe rights (if they had any), it being of the utmoſt conſequence to the enjoyment of their *own* mines to have the dominion of this place, in order to free thoſe mines from water That the ore raiſed within the paſture was of very conſiderable value, and at all events profitable to the lord, this will be the firſt branch of my evidence I ſhall then proceed to prove to you, the uſe and enjoyment of the paſture as a ſeperate property, previous to the purchaſe, and during the whole of Harker's poſſeſſion, as far as the memory of witneſſes will reach I will call all the family of Harker that are yet alive, by ill fortune two or three are dead ſince the laſt trial, but, by good fortune, enough are left to prove thoſe facts I will call all the family of Metcalf, of Scot, who ſucceeded Metcalf, all Tenants of the farm, and they will tell you what was their uſe, and what they underſtood to be their right I will call to you witneſſes

nesses to prove the hounding and herding of cattle from off the place in question I will prove to you that Harker was called upon by the agents of the duke of Wharton to repair his fences, that he pleaded his inability, unless they would allow him a year's rent, that Harker turned off Metcalfe's sheep, and that, as soon as Metcalfe had an opportunity, when he became the tenant, he in like manner turned off even those of Harker I will prove that so far from its being an accidental thing, or that he hounded only out of his other grounds, that he (Harker) hounded very roughly from off the ground in dispute, he drove the sheep down the scars, and the owners complained of his breaking their necks, that there was a general assembly of the tenants of Stonesdale, Ivelet, &c that they had in contemplation to bring an action against him, not for the purpose of asserting their right to this place as a common, but for his not keeping his fences in repair, and hounding their sheep in the severe manner he did I will prove, that with regard to all these tenants who are said to have exercised a right of common without interruption, that they have applied to Harker, they have begged he would snap only one dog, and drive their sheep more tenderly, that they owned they were all at his mercy I will prove that he has taken in cattle to agist, and that it was an avowed right in Harker, and the received opinion throughout the country, that he had such right equal with any other farmer in the country: I shall then, in the last place, call all the witnesses who speak of the repairs of the fence, the manner in which they were done I shall prove they were not made by Mr. Parkes, but repaired by the steward, Mr Wilson, at the request of the tenant, for the purpose of the farm, that they were paid for by him, that in repairing the fences he followed the line of the old wall, that he made no new work, but went where the other had gone before.

Now, gentlemen, when I have proved what I have stated to you, I shall then have a good right to say, that the cause comes before you for your judgment, exactly upon the same evidence that it was tried by the former jury, who passed their verdict upon it For after I have established this case, after I have proved the possession from the year

 1738,

1738, both as to the mines and the pasture, without interruption; after I have proved the state and condition of the fences, I shall be extremely indifferent, whether the two papers, that were with so much exultation produced on Saturday night, were ever given into court or not, they cannot weigh a feather in this cause. The question to be tried is not what this pasture was in 1636, it is not a question which we are to have recourse to antiquarians to decide, the single question is, what was included in Mr Smith's purchase, *that* is to be proved by the possession given *at the time* of the purchase, and the enjoyment *since*.

I cannot, however, pass over the *introduction* of these papers without some little observation upon them, they were brought in at the very close of the evening, they were read, not objected to, I do not know that any objection lies to them, I am very little acquainted with what they are, I took some minutes of them as they were read in court When I went out of court, I desired to have copies of these papers, and did hope to have had them in time to have made some observations upon them, and to have had the assistance of the learned gentlemen engaged in this cause with me, we had a meeting yesterday at one o'clock, the copies had been promised by Lord Pomfret's solicitor, they were several times sent for, and Mr Smith's solicitor went and compared the copies with the originals, but instead of delivering them, as was fully expected, they declined it, we sent again, and then the copies were flatly refused, and we were told the court had not ordered them I literally and *bona fide* speak to your lordship and the jury, from such observations on those papers as I made in court on Saturday night, at one o'clock on Sunday we met, the copies were absolutely refused, after that, late in the evening, when it could not serve the purpose of our meeting, and when, I do upon my honor assure your lordship, they could be of no use to me, they were brought to Mr Smith's solicitor, he thought it his duty to bring them to me, I then said I would not take the copies, they could be of no use to me

LORD

Lord MANSFIELD. My copy did not come *till* the evening.

MR SOLICITOR GENERAL. The copies were made in the morning, and exiſted at the time we ſent for them.

LORD MANSFIELD. Certainly I would have ordered that you ſhould have had copies, could I have ſuppoſed they would have made a difficulty of delivering them to you.

MR SOLICITOR GENERAL. I know your lordſhip meant to order it, I had not an idea there could have been the leaſt heſitation about it.

MR ATTORNEY GENERAL. When I went out of court, I gave directions that they ſhould have copies.

MR SOLICITOR GENERAL. I have no doubt but the Attorney General's directions, and thoſe of every counſel in the cauſe, would have been to give us copies, but Lord Pomfret's agents thought otherwiſe, and gave a flat denial.*

LORD MANSFIELD. The copies ſeem to be made with a correctneſs that requires an examination with the original, the copies are *fac ſimile* copies, my brother Willes mentions to me that he took away one copy that belonged to the council.

MR WALLACE. That copy, my Lord, was not intended for us.

LORD MANSFIELD. But that was taking away one copy from them.

MR SOLICITOR GENERAL. I urge it no further, I ſay no more about it, but deſire that it may ſtand as an apology for me, if I ſtate any thing incorrect about theſe papers.

---

* *Probably by this time Mr Chaytor had found out his miſtake, and, being aſhamed of his boaſted productions, was unwilling to have them any further examined into.*

LORD

LORD MANSFIELD That paper you ſtated very correctly

MR SOLICITOR GENERAL As to theſe papers, it is indeed a little neceſſary to inquire in what manner they were found, and by *whom* produced, and though I think there is no objection to their being admitted, yet, becauſe a paper may be admitted without objection, it does not follow, that it ſhould be admitted without enquiry, it is always neceſſary to authenticate them Whence come they? what are they? I am told they are part of the Wharton papers relative to this eſtate, where come they from? where is this repoſitory of the Wharton papers kept? is it kept for the benefit of the ſeveral purchaſers? no, it is kept at the earl of Pomfret's at Windſor, who is repreſentative of the vendors of thoſe very eſtates I am certain no purchaſers of any part of the Wharton eſtates can hold themſelves ſecure while lord Pomfret and Mr Chaytor have poſſeſſion of this *Pandora's box*. If theſe papers relate to the title, why are they not given to the different purchaſers of thoſe eſtates, to whom they certainly belong. Gentlemen, *who* found theſe papers? Mr Chaytor, one who has been *unaccountably* active in this cauſe I know he is a gentlemen of an ancient family in the county of York, he once attended the bar, but I believe he has found that the *lead* we deal in, in Weſtminſter Hall, was not ſo profitable as the lead that was found in Bel ly Hill *How* he has been connected with this cauſe I will not now repeat, *the ſtories on that head the country has heard ſufficiently of*, I muſt however ſay, I wiſh ſome other perſon had attended the inſpection of theſe papers along with Mr Chaytor Need I aſk the queſtion? had Mr Chaytor found a paper which made for Mr Smith, would he have produced it? Do you think, upon ſuch an examination of theſe papers, that there would have been a fair production of them on both ſides? Lord Wharton was an accurate man, there may be many reaſons why this piece of ground was not included in the eſtimate they have produced, but if there had been buſhels of papers that would have ſhewn theſe reaſons, they would not have been produced by *Mr Chaytor* But, gentlemen, is the title of a purchaſer to be affected by ſuch a paper as this? for

even

even admitting it to be of great antiquity, yet it is not a record, but merely a paper found upon a search made by Mr Chaytor among the papers of a vendor who has made reserves upon his estate, and produced against a *bona fide* purchaser But, gentlemen, what is this paper of Mr Chaytor's? if I understand it right, it is supposed to be an estimate made by lord Wharton of the value of his estate, it is no *rental*, it is nothing to *charge* his steward, or which could affect any third person, it is certainly no *particular* made by him for the sale of his estates, it is not made as introductory to any bargain between landlord and tenant, it is merely a computation of some kind, but yet *such* a computation as ought not, nay, cannot affect a purchaser, must we necessarily suppose that this paper contains, in point of quantity, all the parcels of ground that this farm then consisted of? it states the farm then to consist of 104 acres, in point of fact it consisted of 150 acres, exclusive of the place in dispute, but to solve that, they say the acres are computed ones, then they draw the inference, that computed acres, like computed miles, are one third more I have a right to suppose they were field acres, if so, I know those are one third less, instead of more, but all this is mere guess work, it may be very ingenious, but God forbid that all this ingenuity of guessing should affect a purchase after a possession of thirty years

I will, gentlemen, for argument's sake, admit that this place was formerly part of the waste of the manor, and yet are we to suppose that no title could be gained by any person to it as a private separate possession? if this argument prevails against such a possession as I shall prove, if against the evidence of the actual separate usage and enjoyment cotemporary to the purchase, any stress is laid upon such papers as these, no title is safe, no property is secure, the consequences of such a fatal principle are not confined to this cause, nor to the single subject of this dispute.

I observed, gentlemen, that Nan Intake (which is indisputably a part of East Stonesdale farm) is, from the name, supposed by the other side

side to have been part of the wastes We are told by the witnesses, that the fences of that place are in as bad a condition as the fences round this pasture, I believe they may The next attempt to be made by lord Pomfret will be at Nun Intack, and it is not the first time we have heard that the commoners would be instigated and supported to bring actions to assert a right to that place

It is not, gentlemen, the property of Mr Smith alone that is at stake, but all the property in the kingdom, if, by means of such loose papers as these, any estate can be proved to have been once a part of the common, the ground must be laid open to the common again, that is the inference that must necessarily follow, it is not confined to Mr Smith, and the other purchasers of the Wharton estate, but the property of all the gentlemen in the county of York, and the neighbouring counties, wherever there has been a moor, stands on the most feeble, the most tottering foundation that can possibly be imagined There is a gentleman, known to most of us who have gone the northern circuit, Mr Graham, I beg leave to ask what was the condition of his cultivated fields in 1636 ——If such boxes are to be searched and ransacked, if they are to be let loose upon a *bona fide* purchaser, the condition of his property is even worse than natural accidents can make it, Solway Moss is not so bad, so dreadful as that tremendous box that is kept by lord Pomfret and *searched by Mr Chaytor*, vulcanos, hurricanes, tempests, earthquakes, are not more pernicious, and if such papers are to be kept up, and then produced at the most distant period, to undermine a title, the lands in Yorkshire, which are now worth forty years purchase, will not be worth more than lands in the most desart parts of the kingdom If such a possession, as I have opened and shall prove, will not defend your property, it is in vain to add years to years, not even centuries will insure your estates, they lie equally at the mercy of every invader, and if it was possible to pay the least attention to *such* papers, the best lesson and the best law you could learn by this journey to London, would be, to sell your estates in Yorkshire, put your money in the funds where neither lord Pomfret nor Mr Chaytor could attack what

you

you have in your poſſeſſion, and would wiſh to leave to your poſterity, as their inheritance

I have gone through my obſervations on *Mr. Chaytor's papers*, and treated them with far more attention than they deſerved— I have often heard it laid down, that againſt the lord of a manor, and even againſt a claim of the crown, ſuch poſſeſſion as I have ſtated, and ſhall undoubtedly prove, ought always to prevail, I aſk no more in the preſent caſe than that it ſhould prevail againſt the vague imagination that this place is a part of the waſtes, and againſt idle concluſions of God knows what, ariſing from papers produced *God knows from whence*, all I ſhall now ſay is, what I began with, and with which I ſhall cloſe, "I will prove the enjoyment of this paſture previous to, and at the time of the purchaſe, I will prove how it was held by the tenant in whoſe occupation it was deſcribed to be when Mr. Smith bought it, I will prove it by every act of poſſeſſion, both above ground and below, from the time of the purchaſe to the commencement of this diſpute, and I think when this is done, I have a right to ſay boldly and confidently of the truth of this cauſe (if I may be allowed to borrow a ſacred expreſſion) that "*The gates of hell ſhall not prevail againſt it*."

F I N I S.

www.ingramcontent.com/pod-product-compliance
Ingram Content Group UK Ltd.
Pitfield, Milton Keynes, MK11 3LW, UK
UKHW020822290926
15470UKWH00003B/1306